SEVEN HORN ELEGY

Ishmael Fiifi Annobil

TOTEM

Publishers of Contemporary Literature and Art

THE AUTHOR

ISHMAEL FIIFI AYEREBI ANNOBIL was born in 1958, at Kaneshie, Accra, Ghana. He started writing poetry at the age of eleven, having been inspired by the Ghanaian Avant Garde poets of the sixties and seventies, especially Atukwei Okai, and gained early membership of the prestigious National Association of Writers (NAW).

He entered journalism soon after high school, working on the Ghanaian national newspaper, Daily Graphic, as a proof reader and freelance reporter. He emigrated to East Africa in 1982, armed with an unprecedented testimonial from NAW.

He lived in the Sudan (Juba) briefly, and in Kenya (Nairobi), where he worked as a journalist and collected his poetry; culminating in his writing and performing of the acclaimed recital, *Criers on The Thresholds of Reality* - (Nairobi 1983) - a pioneering multi-media presentation, employing his poetry and drumming, and kinematic projections of fine art pieces by Kenyan artist, Bethuel Alunga Omolo. The show's success attracted, simultaneously, a travel award from the Kenya-Arab Friendship Association, to tour all Arab countries, and an invitation to join the staff of *Kenya Business Spotlight* as an arts and economic affairs correspondent. He chose the latter, moving to England the same year, where he was subsequently appointed deputy editor of a London based diaspora publication. He moved to Wales with his family in 1987.

Annobil was educated at Christian Methodist Secondary School (Ghana), and studied Social- Anthropology briefly at Goldsmith's College (London). He has read and published his poems in numerous places and publications in Africa and the UK. His poem *Aqua Lumina* inspired a public sculpture by American installation artist, Suzy Sureck, for New York's Socrates Park (September 1996).

His English language writing captures the complex, higher structures of African language, philosophic thought, and expression, that underpin Africa's unparalleled gift for all languages, scholarship, diplomacy, oratory, poetic fervour, rhythm, tenacity, fearlessness, inner-joy, giving, forgiveness, and charismatic spirituality.

Annobil is the founder/artistic director of the Welsh based international poetry festival, *Iolo's Children*, and the founder/editor of the international arts newspaper, *Circa21*. He is also a short story writer, novelist, publisher, critic, painter, graphic designer and inventor.

He lives in Cardiff, Wales, with his wife, Helen, and their two young children, Brendan and Vanessa.

First published in Wales (UK) 1988 by TOTEM
55 Merches Gardens, Cardiff, Wales, Britain CF1 7RF

Title: Seven Horn Elegy / *Subject*: Poetry
Author: Ishmael Fiifi Ayerebi Annobil / *Nationality* :Ghanaian
Descent: Fanti and Ga

ISBN 1899151-00-1 (Paperback)

Designed and Typeset by Papyrus-Ibis

Cover illustration by Vanessa Yaa Annobil
(from the Ashanti philosophic emblem, *Nkyimkyim* - Transmutability)

Background Motif (cover): detail from Author's Father's
Akwajang (or robe) © Vlisco, Veritable Wax Hollandais
F.A. Annobil's Portrait: by Emma Lawton
J.Q. Annobil's Portrait: by Anon. Photographer (Ghana)
© The Estate of J.Q. Annobil

*Published with the financial support of the
Arts Council of Wales*

Printed in Wales (UK) by
Barry Advertiser, Watson Street, Barry, South Glamorgan CF63 4EQ

ACKNOWLEDGEMENTS

Many of the pieces in this collection were first read at
Iolo's Children Poetry Festival, Cardiff ('93 & '94)
and at sessions at the *Undercover Poets* (now, *Working Title Poets*) club,
Cardiff, where one enjoys the verve of Canadian Poet, Kerry-Lee Powell.

Seven Horn Elegy was first read at *Site-Ations 1995* (Cardiff) to an
international audience of installation artists.
Letter To Dafydd was first read at the
Dylan Thomas Centre (Ty LLen), on 31st Oct. 1996, in the company of
the brilliant Ghano-Jamaican poet Kwame Dawes.
Silhouette first appeared in Eugene Nowakowski's *Cardiff Poets*.
Oral History and *Zoologised* were first published in the *Yellow Crane*.
The poems *Spirits*, *Mother's Burden*, *Ozonia* and *Triad Spirits* were
written to accompany paintings by the Kenyan 'abstra-realist',
Bethuel Alunga Omolo, with whom I produced the inspired
Criers On The Thresholds Of Reality (Nairobi '83).

Aqua Lumina II was abstracted from my original, *Teardrop-Aqua Lumina*,
which I wrote on 9/8/95 and dedicated to New York installation artist,
Suzy Sureck. I carried out this abstraction on 11th July 1996 for Suzy's
sculpture for Socrates Park, Fall 1996, which she'd named for the poem.
Sadly, by dubious default , the New York Times' review of the project
entombed my piece as: "...a poem", and granted me anonymity -
I therefore state, for the sake of posterity, my own acknowledgement of
that so-called collaborative process, while asserting my ownership
of the title: Aqua Lumina.

I acknowledge my wife, Helen, as the best critic I have ever had.
Credits are due to Brendan, my 13 year old son, for casting his invaluable
critical eye over the artistic options that arose in the making of this book.
I owe my daughter ,Vanessa, credit for the title of the poem,
Water On The Sky, which she ventured at the tender age of 4 yrs, and
for the cover illustration for this book, at the age of 11 yrs !

The glossary/exegesis of Seven Horn Elegy has benefited greatly from the
authoritative glossary of *Lorgorligi Logarithms*, the trail blazing collection
by my mentor, the great Ghanaian avant garde poet, Atukwei Okai...
To you, Atukwei, I have to say: Between your *Lorgorligi* and the
Dreamdom Communique, I heard the calling.

I acknowledge with thanks the anonymous Arts Council of Wales' reader,
for recommending this book for grant support.

I acknowledge the original, Christian African peoples of Sudan, amongst
whom I sojourned, for teaching me about *the* real dignity,
and for waking up the surrealism in me - I'll respect you forever!

GRATITUDE

My Sincerest Thanks To:

My Dear , Late Sacrificial Mother , HANNAH AKU GBERBIE,
who breathed God into me;
My kind Wife, HELEN,
and our great children , BRENDAN AND VANESSA;
My Sister and Brothers, 'SISTER', ENOCH , AFERI,
Bro ODARTEY, Bro OKO & KUUKU, especially Enoch for giving me
the chance to travel; My good nephew, EUGENE ;
my gracious in-laws, MARY and MAURICE JACKSON,
and the entire families
JACKSON, BOYE, OMOLO, COLLIS, BELLAMY, GEORGE;
Mrs FLORENCE OMOLO of Nairobi, who called me son
and named me *Omuothrese* (Comforter);
SUE and BOB HUNT of Maesycoed (Wales) who helped
in harsher times; IFOR THOMAS, for his pure humanity;
NICKY DELGADO,for sharing ; RODDY DUNCAN, for insight
The Late JOE AMARTEY, classmate, friend and fellow journalist;
SELASSIE GARD, SAMANTHA KUSI, and all the GARDS;
Mrs. NIMAKO and Mrs. MENSAH, the Teachers
who saw past my truancy.

Also to NATURE,
for my timely awareness of the World's Poor ;
YILMAZ GUNEY, a true Kurd, filmmaker and Martyr;
MARTIN LUTHER KING, GHANDI, KENNEDY and LINCOLN ;
The Aboriginal Peoples of Australia ,The Americas & Africa;
The peerless Geniuses:
Dr. KWAME NKRUMAH and Dr. KWEGYIR AGGREY;
The Profound, Exciting Intellect of GHANAIANS;
And
My living or departed HEROES, and the FRIENDS, who have
unwittingly incited my finest poetic responses:
ATUKWEI OKAI
Miles Davis, Mohammed Ali
Toni Morrisson, Maya Angelou, Isaac Bashevis Singer,
Saul Bellow, Gabriel Garcia Marquez, Rubadiri,
Fela, C.K. Mann, Ampadu, Haendel, Ephraim Amu,Thom,
Joe Achana, Christopher Mulei, Kafka, Thomas Rain Crowe,
Iolo Morganwg, Paul Robeson, Mogg Williams, Paul P. Piech, Bob Mole,
Peter Finch, Ifor Thomas, Tôpher Mills, Kaite O'Reilly, Richard Gwyn
JESUS

CONTENTS

**Dedicated to the Beloved Memory of my Father
JACOB QUAO ANNOBIL**

PROLOGUE

These are true images of our times. I have painted what I know. I have consorted with the common atavism of the human race as well as a certain latent vigour within my Ghanaian culture - That vigour which transpires traditionally as a hedge- expression, unpredictable, avoiding the epicentre of popular thought, and yet informing it - as is manifest on the tongue of the storyteller fronting the midnight convention of light:

He /she has walked the dewy fringes of time and garnered arcane truths, so he /she entices us in turn on a walk along the fringes of our minds, to a sacred discovery ; coaxing our awe, jolting our hearts with his /her nuance, and deft musical 'entrements', of which we gladly partake, till he/she merges with the constellation of fireflies. Thence he/she is ethereal, defying recognition, making our skins creep with fear's spasm, till we are unable to turn our heads and look behind us, lest we face our other selves in the dark. We are transfixed; indentured by an irrevocable truth, begotten by the oracles.

Seven Horn Elegy represents the compassion, passion and defiance that characterised the spirit of my Late father, the prince who refused to be enstooled the **Twafohene** of **Winneba**. In mourning him therefore, I must also lament the plight of the world's disadvantaged, for whom he greatly cared, and pay due homage to the land that has abided my most meaningful artistic phase and communion, Wales.

The title here adopted is duly excised out of **Mmenson**, the Ashanti seven-horn dirge, that elevates the passage of kings.

Above all, as an African, I will not deny the invisible wings that swoon down and flutter about me, whenever I approach doom, and so I credit this entire collection to The Almighty.

i . ƒ . a. a.
(Cardiff 1998)

IX

SPIRITS

A pensive glow:
Awe's ethereal inhabitants.

Who gave birth to umbilical cord -
Where did it go?

Spring 1992, Pontypridd, Wales.

MOTHER'S BURDEN

Ruptured emblem:
Dissembling in good,
A pout, our foul pout
Toothed upon two
Alveolate sparks.

A withered victim, still
Facing her silhouette ... still.

Spring 1991, Pontypridd, Wales.

THE TRANSIENCE

Cloisters of monkeys
Verdigris fountains,
Moss, fertile with
Drosophila and skinks - the sanctum.

Serenity dwells here:
The pit of a slowed elbow
Plugged with wet
Nutmeg and myrrh.

Discarded schnapps-
A failed oblation
To an expectation;
The jingling of a
Phantasmic manifest -

Mere memories on papyrus.

It has passed on now,
Blasted out of its void
Failed even by the wake's
Attentiveness.

The replacements
Are already yelling
To the midwife's
Prompting tap;

Some to vacate their voids
early...

All ingrained
By their earthly deeds -
Cicatrix in molten magma.

Transient awes.

26/4/92 Tonteg, Wales.

THE METROPOLIS

Flickering brown eyes,
A cheery 'madman',
African - a distant
Relative of a town
Somewhere, dimmed
To his conscience.

He wears a coat of
Many pockets, stuffed
As if in haste
With debris for
A magpie's nest.

He in his numb
State simplifying
Life's exigencies -
A leering metaphysical
Giant of innocence.

He bears on,
On the parallel.

24/3/92 Cardiff-Tonteg (BEBB Bus)

For the Humpback Whale

WATER ON THE SKY

Join me on this walk to
The seven oracles

You may come aproned,
Cleaver in hand,
Even a dog to guard your dreams.

I shall take you to
See them,
The oracles;
Grindstones, millers of yesteryear,
You'll see, bring your cleaver.

We shall sail over each
Wet hump, and slash
Its back with your favourite cleaver,
Slash and slash.

Our tables shall be full
Forever, please come along,
They are wasting.

No? Don't mind the bloodbath.
Are you that squeamish, dearie?
You shock me!

The oracles merely want an
Audience with the soul-dead.
They collect your kind of flesh.

27/12/91 Tonteg, wales

15

For Ghandi, Luther King, Kennedy and Lincoln

THE HAND

Soothsayers entranced
In a giddy omen,
Trampolined forth.

Pronouncing the dream! -

Albatrosses emanated
From the near fictive mind
Onto a sinking shipsdeck.

The dream ... then the woe:

A blanketed hand, one-prong
In a nook corner of a chronicle -
A slow cold caress - a dark
Flame...

Incubus is found sucking
The 'carrion' dry; still
Burdened with the stubborn carcass
Of a dhoti-clad
        god.

20/12/91 Tonteg, Wales

SILHOUETTE

A slow march,
Agitated by flies:
The crevices are full
Of honeybees that love carcasses:

A samsaran ritual
Animated by an ego;

The sandhoppers are
Lipsticked, drunk
In the mellow fugue:
Sanguine;
Chained in the stretto of bones
 forever.

22/12/91 Tonteg, Wales

For Rwanda

ORAL HISTORY

Finish your meal
Before long,
For you may yet
Be betrayed by guns
And have to run
Into oblivion on an
Empty belly.

Oblivion is a
Volcanic mat
That fails to
Sprout the clay
That made us.

Oblivion is a
Primeval trek
Caged in by scorpions
That ride the backs of
Crabs
In the dark.

Finish your meal
Before long, my child,
And tie the crumbs
To your ankles
For you may yet
Be herded off
To die on a graveless
Plateau.

15/8/94 Grangetown, Cardiff

WEATHER CLOCK SOLILOQUY

London is a soliloquy...
A weather clock that never
Shines on Sunday alas
The swallows eat droppings
At low perched old palms

Believe me the swallows
Shivered last winter till
Their hearts dropped dead
        embalmed
In oxfam soup.

Then soliloquy patted himself.

Autumn 1987, Wales-bound, Intercity train

For the Masai

ZOOLOGISED

He stood against the sun
Brazened to his earlobes,
Vultured by norm.

A pot in the making, they say,
Gyrated upright for the
Tender touch of master's fingers;

Such pots rise high
Toughened with the grit
Of swallowed angst.

Bwana, the sisal-king,
A ludicrous potter with
His coy-affected head
Between his own buttocks,

Fetching the stiff end
Of the worm that ate his molars;

A whisk in hand,
He orders the brazened pottery
To the zoo.

27/12/91 Tonteg, Wales

RWANDA

Toadstools grow
In their nostrils -
Poisoned, the soldiers -

Bats,
pressed to
The red glint of
Blades of an
Apocalypse.

The day the sun
Fell into
The river - the rainbow is off colour -
The penumbra wept
Red tears

and howled.

20/5/94 Grangetown, Cardiff

ABANKABA

You prefer him on a long, long road, signposted
blank, with windy sediments;

Attended by a dancing mirage, and a
Stark chaperon: an elbow cooled
In brine, callused with use.

He should drink of your
Puerile acidity, punctured into
A whirlwind of change ~ why.

Or does his mystique haunt you?

22/12/91 Tonteg

OZONIA

Misty sizzle of waves
Gnarling the gondola's
Gilded frontispiece ~ She
The Gondolier steered de-eyed
Past quandary's wall to
Golgotha, on golem's heels.

Spring 1991, Pontypridd, Wales

For the displaced and itinerant

VANISHED WORLDS

A creaking, cringing
Cavalcade...
sailing the dusk
of civilization.

Then an eerie tallyhoo ~ tallyhoo

Loitering emotions jiggled
Into mud,

Goaded to the ravine
Where corn grows wild, a
campfire,
                Feared.

                ...tallyhoo ~ tallyhoo

Sonorous reflexes abide time;
Remit hate.

Till
A cremated
Phoenix rises ~ only head-high.

19/12/91 Tonteg, Wales

LAVABO

A sun backed mountain-top
Above an Appalachian palm

    Soaring eagles here may forego a
    Rectal flinch:

A plummeting silver coin
On a large silver platter.

The palm is washed to please
The giver - the giver's
Thoroughly washed, if of soiled flesh,

    In a deep tankard of acid.

19/12/91 Tonteg

For the homeless

ICE

An effigy is soaked under
A gaudy rotunda, in haste;

Cold sweltered dishes
Leer past his-her septum,
Curled up by a peel
Of lemon - frothy cocktail
On a peacock's caudal fin.

He-she fingers own faeces and licks its shadow.

"...Is the thing normal?", they ask,

Those lilting contrived tongues,
Clicking austere heels
Twirling on insensate affability
Mimicking a period piece; reflecting
Dickensian counterpoints with
Mezzo dexterity:

To each protagonist, he-she is the
Soiled spoiler of humanity - they flee.

He-she sits: a totem pole anointed
With broken eggs, squashed
Pasties, crumbs from sufficient gods:
Libations to the decapitated.

The janitor's broom breaks it free at last,
An ice sculpture: icicled eyelashes
Still begging our underfoot
To avoid the discarded,
Defunct coin.

The unknown soon thaws underfoot,
Frittered - a blank stamp
Torn off a serrated edge
To wrap up a shivering undertaker's dream.

20/12/91 Tonteg

For Yilmaz Guney

KURDS

Indiscreet yawn

[Pallid fears, moon's horns
And a catapult]

Was it a yawn at all
Indiscreet like that;
Or was it stupor's gape?

Slurry and felled limbs;
Holy beards
Of chieftains,
Contorted by a lewd
Quake of mind.

        Lopsided shelters
Perched as if by vertigo
Near death's well.

Their tears are frozen
To their cheeks
Like scales of stretched
Calluses, dignity
Obliqued by the agony of
wailings and wailings-

[A chilled wind
Brocaded by strobed fire
And gnawing echoes]:

Here we are again, a mutilated child
Suckling on a torn heart
In mummy's
Trembling arms - she a martyr

Her baby mumbles a discreet farewell,
Watching, watching, watching you.

November 1992 Cardiff

AFRICA IN YOUR EYES

B-girl
The geneticist's pregnant mare:
Getter of anxiety's altruism

Luscious honey dame
Astraddle a bar stool,
Pantyless; skirt rolled back,
Groaning with the slurping
Of tongues.

Anubis of a living world,
Sniffing the winds for
Ripe groins -
Giver of sedate oracles.

29/12/91 Tonteg

HOME

A pretty faced fate,
Land of ancient myth
And yellowed pages.

Slanting spearheads
All leaning to catch
A foreign bayou
That never empties
Its bounty
Into your river.

Still the trains carry their golden fare
To sea, past your wharfs
That settle the egos of peacocks.

Our generation is in bed
Touching itself under
A cold blanket,
While you weep all day long,
Pretty faced fate, to be taken,
Raw and unfettered.

The trains still carry their dusty fare
To sea, past your wharfs
That settle the palates
Of limbo dancers and prostitutes.

We are leaving you.
Pray
Pray
We remember you.

15/8/94 Grangetown, Cardiff

For Iolo Morganwg (a song for Wales)

LETTER TO DAFYDD

I don't recall
The face in the mist.

Pummelled of light -
A fishbone cast in forgotten clay;

It doesn't answer me -
Dafydd, I keep on shouting,
Dafydd...you Dafydd, I call you.

A beleaguered face
Staring askance at my tears...
Dafydd. if it's you
Then say the password, let's clench hands.
It's simple, Dafydd:
Yours is the sweeter word.

I say mine in English
And you say yours in ...
Remember?

Why do you turn away
When I look for your eyes?
Or are you scandalised
By the straw of light between us?...

No - It's not you Dafydd,
Not usually mute.
It's not Dafydd, alright -
Not usually shy either.

Is it the scar?
Is it that nasty scar
You are hiding from me? Dafydd?
Is it the scar from the childhood
Joust we had,
In that summery month
Before that terrible winter
Rotted our teeth?

Perhaps you don't
Understand my language.
Don't you?
Yes, I lost the oratory
But my soul still sings
With fibre from this soil - this soil!
Not some prostituted sonority
Cast this side
Of their table.

I don't eat crumbs. remember?
Nor sing them either...
Just...come...out...of...that...mist..now!

But he stays on behind
The mist, languid and wise
Like a Rebecca...pummelled
Of light, mesmerising,
And accusing like
A miller's crushed finger.

There is a distance, yes,
But I still love you.
All I want is that
Chilling call of yours
So that I may mourn you again, Dafydd.

Yet reluctantly do I ask
For that call, for
If you do call me
I shall cry with
The pain of your past.

You are blessed with all the keys
To my hidden soul,
And you know it
- I love peace.

But watch this land of yours, Dafydd,
Watch it carefully - it's new.
Let it pray to you
Let it wash your feet
Walk her cobbled back

To pluck back the feather
...We lost in the storm.
I may not have your oratory anymore
But I am trumpeting anyhow.

I am sat at our
End of the tunnel
Trumpeting to them
As they speed past me.
And I tell them this:

"I may seem like a cave, almost
Hollow and dank with flintstones
For conscience...
I may even seem to play the redoubt to
The muffled dreams of your yearning souls...
But mystique is mine, only mine".

They don't listen, Dafydd.

Is it really you?
A face in a mist,
Watching askance as
I play out my repentance
Under this downy blanket?
You are watching me
like a mother...

Will you step out of that
Bloody mist, Dafydd,
And take my shivering
Hand between your
Strong jaws!

Summer 1995, Grangetown, Cardiff

SNAPSHOTS OF A TIME KNOWN

Inclined dolls
Verging on the wind
To take a peck from

The offal eaters:
Bistro-bound, with bellow-like
Dewlaps - targets of
Their love hate.

Greased lips in candlelight
Kneading hairy ears
Of atrophied heads, maggoty.

The lull: orgasmic guffaws are heightened
For a moment   then

A cascade of dolls
Steals the peepshow's guests.

Shillingi imbili * becomes a
Precious talisman to
Empty palms.

11/1/92 Tonteg

* (East Africa- Swahili) Literally, Two Shillings

JOY

Slash of fever, goosepimply like
A repoussé cauldron,
Suspended.

A hamstring on pain's horn.

Equilibrium of
Our duality - momentary...

Like the noon before
The creaky minaret undermines
The muezzin's hafizic idyll.

20/12/91 Tonteg

34

WHAT THE HELL

Are we to hate
Our lots or selves

When the obeah
Beats the cracked gong
At our door

Are we to fight
Or submit
Like sheep, staring
Our slayer from the corner
Of one eye, while
The other drowns
In our blood

Are we to run
And run, till
Our songs light up
The caves

Are we?

November 1992 Cardiff

JAZZ
[In Three Movements]

I
INNUENDO

Push all of
Yesterdays
Over to me -

The cobwebs
The yellowing brocade
Discarded years
Rusting rags and sunflowers
Mothed velvets
The sunsets
The autumns
Clay fetishes
Curios of exotica
Effigies of history
Tajmahal, soundfever
Writs of mandamus and
Habeas corpus

Funk and jazz
Blues, miles D, dizzy G
And sunRa, jimmy H
The faculty of modern arts
Wavelets of the southern vectis
Africa's dawns and dusks
creaky sutra

Leave out the drugs.

II
OCHRE (*for Accra*)

Arrested sundial:
Kpokpoi is the food
Of dominant souls.

Count in terracotta,
The sepia cards
That hold the past.

Upright Navrongo gourd of *pito*
Dominant aqua

The anthills of
Your plains
The dust of sweat

Pesewas of paper
Worn close to the
Market woman's waistline.

III
SUNRAY PASTORALE (*for Aburi*)

Avuncular (uncle)
Protégé and ... 'gée

Crystalline dot
...esque and dewdrops

Titian mirrors
Image coinage
Parti-colour genii

Runcible spoon

Glint of solarium
Peevish telephone

Rounded back of
Receding *otofo*

Prone quill, centrestage.
Talcum powder,
Mere talcum powder for the flunkey.

Perfumed rococo limbs.

21/1/92 (Tonteg) and 6/10/92 (Grangetown, Cardiff)

38

AQUA LUMINA II
(Incantation for water)

Aqua
Lumina

Flower
of
Deserts

Mirror
of
Saints

Vortex
of
Enigma

Teardrop
of
Ancestry

Swift allure

~

Sing

11/7/96, Grangetown, Cardiff

For Emma Lawton

ACROTER

Curvatures
Of light.

The dawn's piquant
rust,
clay;
impending ~

Zen vignettes;
vignettes and
the

Unsoiled vestibule;
passage to
the vestry of eons,
dew-glass, more ordered *banquettes*;

Blue glass conscience
...telepathy.

The floating orb,
A sturdy eyeball,
Stays at your fingertip;
tensed by a singular urge:

Resurrection!

A wailing garden
parts for angels to enter the prayer

*(You unhinged your window
long, long before this dawn)*:

We still see
the sweet jingle of stones
kissed by them, only them.

25/2/97- 12.25am, Grangetown, Cardiff

ASHI

You fitted in briefly
Only when it suited
Our delinquency - you
Had the mantle then:

The billowing cover cloth
Over our illicit rebellions:
The holes in walls
That betrayed the self-love
Of estranged wives.

We only knocked
When your street-wisdom
Must yield the victuals
Our mothers withheld
To force our submission.

You also gave the sideshow,
Unschooled as you were,
A clown in collegiate get-up, you
Scored the centrepoint always
...always till
The language moulded
Into that foreign tongue.
Then your pidgin trailed
Sadly, doggedly clawing
The marble sheet of voices
To surrender - it didn't.

We hailed you in
A loud awkward way,
Sure in our
Subconscious sense of
Superiority-

You were the fishmonger's son.

We were, Ashi, the privileged
Revellers at a
Moonlit aboriginal feast;
Liberal to the point
Of orgiastic abandon,
Till the cockcrows
Alerted us.

Then you saw us
Slide off, running past
Your weighted arms;
The skeletons of your
Victuals strewn
On the gutter's edge
To ward off stray dogs.

We had been called
By an inner voice, woken
Like willing zombies
To chalk our stilted fates
In the miasma
We once decried.

You had been used,
And you felt your
Soul starting the
Imminent decline early:

Those users to become
The prides of families
That took no part
In the dark theatre you once led.

We owe you the street-wisdom
But cannot say so.

Today we see your shadow
Here and there struggling
With a different
Life...we toss you

A note of familiarity,
You smile, but like
A disowned father only -
you never made it to sea.

Then I long to be
Teen again, to
Heed your tales of illusion,
The apocryphal tempests,
Beached sea monsters and hammerheads,
That followed your
Borrowed barcarolle
Into our dreams.

11/8/94 Grangetown, Cardiff

SPRING'S DEARTH

Hayfever,
Radio 2 soiree
Past midnight;
You help out with
DJ's trivial-pursuit.

An unearning adult
Postured to conquer
Tedium with pride

Lofty birdcage,
New Yorkers for catharsis
Newsweek for adrenal fix
Saul Bellow for a smile
And the urge to compose.

Poisoned inkpot
Layers of rusty inspiration
Fangs bared to enact
Eponymous diatribes
Against greed and mammon
(*Those that want it hate it*)

You keep keeping the door open
For your timely
Entry, someday.

26/4/92 Tonteg

YULE-LOG

Garland of hollies,
Floating mid-earth, centred
By the storm's eye;

A mulct, dragged out
Of a wilderness,
Trailed by a cornucopia
Of thorns;

To pre-celebrate a mid-sublime
Lynching at past-thirty turns of the
Sundial:

The earth is thus
Impaled, waiting for the wind to clear,
The cockcrows are already done,

The supplicants are passionate,
Frenzied in a foetal yearning.

24/12/91 Shanklin, Isle Of Wight

INKLING

Is it the
Dripping tap

Or the voice
Of restless sleep?

A candid whisper
That flicks the afferent altar

Or is evil the intimate
Noise of darkness,

Are you salt-fish,

Prey to the acrid tongues
That fail in the
Nocturnal
Mission of
Cannibals?

You feel the inkling
Of sulphur in the air-
All night long.

6/10/92 Grangetown, Cardiff

DISTANCES

Uninspired by age.
Their shilling-sized voices
Knocking against the wind.

They are ready to deflower
Any deflowerer -
Still nebulous, nymphal,
These tiny fireflies, yet
Unsteadied by fallopian culture.

They recall the seminal pain,
The gristly pistol that strayed
Into their paths...
All
A distant gut feeling now,
Manipulated by a sleeping
Coxswain.

27/12/91 Portsmouth to Cardiff Train

VACUUM

An implied hello:
A gaudy carnival

Blistered soles
Treading a bloodied
Soil, where stymied
Love once throed

Past now washed doorways
That once spelt neurotic
Messages of supremacy...

Here a livid vacuum dwells
Here the *Ainu* too might have passed
Unpossessed by a sense of being.

An ill-spent hello after all:
A clanging festival of
Hated ahimshas;
    altruism made of pain.

13/4/92 Tonteg, Wales

ABYSS

Every crusader must weep
Sometime,
        Or we shall
Befall him or her.

Tears are our elixir,
Us frazzled vultures.

We like the fluids
Of submission; when,
Indeed, the weeper
Only escapes to a higher
Altar

To mock our emptiness.

20/5/94 Grangetown, Cardiff

A POET

Sentinel of the ferment,
            of passion's
Rage.

Some choose to call you
A madman, lest
They face your poem.

You and God
Are not afraid
Of each other's
Surprises.

Summerfly of broken
Honeycombs,
Crumbseeker at the birdperch
Lest they name you beggar
Too-
Lest they face your poem.

Nazarene of uncharted
Manna,
Wild eagle, scourge
Of the pompous,

A doomed mendicant
Of a disposable
Credo - silences

Silences   utter
Babel of silences

You flourish

And hope you
Die face-down
Lest you face
Your mourners.

23/1/93 Grangetown, Cardiff

THE GREAT DIER

You must be laid
To rest
Under a modest
Gravestone,
In a seagulled corner
Of a primrose
Desert

So that the
Posthumousy may
Overshadow you -
You the victim
Of nostalgia.

You failed to burn the manuscript, didn't you?

Surely an imminent
Relinquisher of
A dissident
Orthodoxy

They awaited you
To cough it
Out in the frigid
Wrench of hypothermia:

They have patience.

12/6/93 Grangetown, Cardiff.

AYELE

Powder faced
Fishmonger.
An early
Riser too.
Masterful *tekler* tie-er.

Daughter of an oblique mason-
Sculptor of many a
Giddy juxtaposition.
But Ayele is a soft soul,
    A crier at night,
A dam of unrequited love,
Lonesome observer at *wato cafe*
Decked to the nines
In sizzling *kaba, anuatre*
And *mankotamankonor* earrings.
    She is a soft soul
Waiting to burst
Her furnace onto you
The brokeman of learning-
Phoney poet of ancestral pride-
She awaits you
On the cool night mattress
To lavish her curves about
Your narrowed hips.

Her tongue is velvet:
Fluid*er* than a word.

23/1/93 Grangetown, Cardiff

(The poetic trance)

THE ARK

We procrastinate on nuance
And play host to the
Somnambulist, instead.

Life's journey after all
Started with
A vacuous yawn
And a tendril,
High tensile conduit
Of a fleeting honeycomb.

You, somnambulist,
With open palms
Are swatting the frippery of cares,
And facing me, your broken mirror,
With a half sentence,
Of which I never knew,
But will finish.

The love chalice floats between us,
Fluid like a down feather, scudding away
From touch, yet welcoming.

We both drink the
Imagined wine, and become
Drunk obelisks.

Listing against our defiances,
We settle our score
With a furious orgasm.

31/5/97 / 3.20pm Grangetown, Cardiff

ITINERANT POET

A trapped dove
Lain on its side
In the snow.

Passers-by pluck a feather
Or two for doffed hats.

Dequilled stump: a frozen
Norm.
Bearer of an ill-fated
Message.

18/2/92 Tonteg, Wales

DIASPORA

(a personal circumstance)

Voice of lilliput
Vulgar defiance-

A slow
Epiphany, guarded
By the censer of atheists

Claustrophobia,
Concentric almost,
Apart from the
Occasional walkies
That stray time.

6/10/92 Grangetown, Cardiff

(for Helen)

SALVOR'S ARIA

If only the artist could hold a palette knife
to your face, he should be faint
with envy.

The watery being you are:
Rippling behind the swift mirror
of our lilied pond, your dorsal fin
inverted so that you may embrace
the falling sun....
     I hear your twirling song rise
     from the calabash that time hides her
     fortunes in.

Spellbinders, sorcerers and plots
do not touch you; you, the goldfish in the shoal.

Is it that you were born with a Trojan talisman
about your head: garland of ether?

Innocents say your song came from the lake of fools,
for they cannot hear it; and that your water is an illusion
made of mere clay and straw -
     Such are the tales,
wispy like bitten tongues, even to their tellers.

But that's the price you pay for mystery.

     I hear you, arc of music.
     Your children shall be called Significance...
     They shall be.

And this song will remain in their orbit.

14/5/98 Grangetown, Cardiff

A FAREWELL

You looked betrayed
By the light,
Your knees knocked now
After a recent missionary fall
On Jehovah's path.

You stood before me,
Long lost son, who would
Take flight again ~ an
Elusive breeze, still unbroken
By nostalgia or
The solemn days and nights
Of birthplace.

My heart-lurch
Was contained,
Unlike yours that never had the puerile need
To fight nature's ways - except
Your shy, knowing blinks;
As though once sacred, you
Were now my bathos - your tears.

But then I said, didn't I?:

"May the Lord bless you, Mama".

You walked through the iron gate with me
After the strong, parting embrace,
Proud as a mornstar,
And waved a triumphant fist
As my taxi struggled past
Your womb.

Conceived 9/7/94, Kaneshie, Accra

For Dada

SEVEN HORN ELEGY

You are here somewhere.

Still guiding my first steps
Like the warthog in your legends
- The nursing sentinel that
Uprooted trees so as to undo
Surprise.

When recent my lewd dream
Pressed my face into the cleavage
Of sacrilege, you tapped me
Where you would have,
Were you still mortal.

It was you, wasn't it?

That silent firmness of yours
That eluded those who indulged
Only in your open tempests, like
Masochists at a taut *sharia*
Festival of blood and scimitar.

That side of you that
Slipped me money
Round Mama's back
When she chose to punish
My impudence
- I the *pocket-lawyer*
That needed to feel the shin
Of justice in all matters of our
Reclusive homestead.

Why we respected each other, I know now:
You gave me all the genes
That matter in battle, the genes
That hate liars,

Liars and the feline shadows
Of those that betray.

Yet there you lay,
Having opted out of glory
For mine to flourish -

(Yes, my day was made, even the mudflats
Admitted water and rippled with the blue
Sky;
The Aztecs came too, to embolden my grip
On our outer cosmos and Iolo's).

Yet there you lay on the bare
Wet floor of the mortuary
As though you were the symbol
Of a decrepit kharma,
Led in cuffs, naked, to writhe.

Yes, I had been told
Of the nature of your departure:
That spirited evacuation of
A true soldier, voluntary like
The pods that green nature's feet.

And though on your day of departure,
Telepathy had caught me
In the middle of my distant pave
And watered my eyes
With a faceless fever of the heart,
I was still none the wiser
To face that sad cushionless
Rendering our nation had made
Of my idol:

The prince of princes.

Even then you stayed undefiled,
Serene as though you'd finally convinced God.
You shimmered in death, Dada,

Like a sanctified black velvet.

Damirifa due
Damirifa due due
Damirifa due

From your transitory palanquin
You whispered messages to me
No other could hear-
God, it felt sanctifying
To stroke your head,
As the clamourings of death's besotted
Rang around us - and you seemed to
Smile.

You smiled. You smiled.

You possessed the souls
Of your army pallbearers
And the buglers sounded
Your Last Respect
Many more times
Than the best generals ever got.

For they too saw in you the
Light that lit up the broken
Mines in the human soul.
Proudly did the men of *Ashiedu Ketekre*
Deck you in the ensign -

You were both the elephant and the antelope

Oboutu ba*
Nkrapong ba
Obutu ba
Obutu ba ekong
Nkrapong kee amer lagmor dzi o lagmor
Obutu kee o lagmor dzer amer lagmor mling
O lagmor e tsa madzii enyor-ee...Oplo Quao!

---

* Most Ga stanzas and lines are tranlsated in subsequent stanzas or lines - see glossary for others (p64)

Winneba came
Accra came
Winneba came
Winneba came again
Accra said their umbilical cord is yours
Winneba said your umbilical cord emerged from theirs
O Your umbilical cord has united two nations!...Oplo Quao!

Yet there were
unfilled places
At our enchanted wake:

They did not come to bid
You farewell, those
Whose barren mouths you
Once watered, those hapless
Children you once rescued from
Treachery and brought home
In your sacrificial rage.

They could not face your glory.

That you defeated satan in
All ways, is our secret,
For you and I were born to
Kiss the tragic ground that
The Messiah walked.

You taught me honour.
You taught me sacrifice.
You taught me inner joy.
You taught me to cry as a man.

And I too have come to
Undress the belaboured litanies
Of gilded apostasy, the fuming
Censers of apostolic
Imposters
That defile the faucet
Our angels sip from.

You are free now,
Free of the remorse of
Discord and betrayal.

You are free to tip the scales
For those you failed
To honour with your might.

You are free to smile
Over the woes that befell us
And broke the family orb.

When I come, I promise, I shall bring
The rest of the glory
You left behind.

But stay close...stay close
To my heart.

Stay and tap me
When my heels
Are tempted to
Flee the shrine

Stay.

Stay, I beg you, stay.

Mantse egboo-eeee-ei, mantse eteshi ekong!
A king has passed on, a king has risen again!

Mmenson blow, blow your hearts out, Mmenson:

Damirifa due
Damirifa due due
Damirifa due.

2/9/94 Grangetown

SILHOUETTE (p17)

Samsaran: adjectival neologism from Samsara (Hinduism and Buddhism), The repeated cycles of birth, suffering, death and rebirth. Used thus in conjunction with 'ritual', war becomes a wilful pagan rite by war mongers; the soldier being the sacrifice.

ABANKABA (p22)

Abankaba: (from contemporary Ghanaian folklore) A destitute hero, akin to Cinderella, only less lucky. Used here to represent the guest races of Europe, the gravity of their perennial problems, including xenophobia, which they counter superbly with a strong awareness of their redoubtable mystique and strength.

LAVABO (p25)

Lavabo: The ceremonial washing of hands (Roman Catholic and Anglican) before the Eucharist. Background to poem: Every Christmas, the President of the USA rides the back of a fast train through the Appalachian Mountains, throwing fancy presents to the labourer communities, still living there in abject poverty, as though they were lepers in medieval times. They are, in this poem, recipients of forcible philanthropy; their giver washing his hands in a deep tankard of acid, to avoid affliction by the penury he abides in them - a wanton self-apotheosis also encountered in more benign form in Weather-Clock Soliloquy (p19).

JOY (p34)

Hafizic: From Hafiz (Persian Arabic), a Moslem who has fully memorised the Koran, also a title of respect for the same.

JAZZ - OCHRE (p36)

Kpokpoi: Also called Kpekple, Sacramental food of the Ga people of Accra, Ghana; main oblation to the gods, and the spirits of the departed. Made of steamed meal of new corn, palm oil and saltpetred okra, it is eaten at *Homowo*, the harvest festival, with bitter herbs and palm soup. The feast is started by a ritual guzzling of kpokpoi by clan stalwarts with girded loins. Reminiscent of the Passover, Homowo is a lasting vestige of the race's Hebraic (Hamitic) roots, reflecting their time in Mesopotamia and before.

Navrongo: A Northern Ghanaian city.

Pito: (Northern Ghana) Sorghum beer.

Pesewa(s): (Ghana) Defunct coinage of Cedi currency, used here for nostalgia.

JAZZ - SUNRAY PASTORALE (p38)

Otofo: (*Adangbe*, Ghana) Ancient rite of passage, or the female subject of the rites. She is paraded through the streets for the attention of would-be suitors, her waistline and joints decked in the most expensive *aggrey* (or Phoenician) beads, her breasts bare, her thighs and arms strewn with emblematic, chalk drawings

THE GREAT DIER (p51)

Posthumousy: Neologism from posthumous. The inference being the organised piety of the trustees of a dead artist's legacy.

AYELE: (p52)

Tekler: (*Ga*, Ghana) Cloth money belt used by market women.

Wato Cafe: An Accra clubhouse, the melting-pot of Ghanaian popular music renaissance of the Sixties and Seventies. Designed as a Mississippi river boat, it held on to its reputation till the late Seventies, then gave in to pedestrian recreation and trade.

Kaba: Ghanaian ladies' attire comprising blouse, skirt and cover cloth. Often used to describe the blouse, only.

Annuatre: (Ga)Perfume or cologne.

Mankotamankonor: (Ga) The coat-of-arms of the Ga nation, depicting an antelope standing on the back of an elephant. Interpretation: power is attainable by wisdom and agility, and not by brute strength.

Brokeman: (Pidgin English) a poor person (also in spirit).

SEVEN HORN ELEGY (p58)

Damirifa...: (Asanti,Ghana) Condolences; offered to the spirit of a departed king.